Dipping *into* Lent

ALAN HILLIARD

Published by Messenger Publications, 2017

ISBN 978 1 910248 88 1
Copyright © Alan Hilliard, 2017
All photographs copyright © Alan Hilliard, 2017

Designed by Messenger Publications Design Department
Typeset in Gill Sans, Didot, Rockwell & Dancing Script
Printed by W &G Baird

Messenger Publications,
37 Lower Leeson Street, Dublin D02 W938
www.messenger.ie

Contents

Introduction

Any expert in communications will tell you that one of the keys to successful communication is knowing your audience. Well, I've broken this rule in this publication. Our world is so incredibly diverse that it is very hard to stick with any one audience, and particularly because my life has many audiences.

These reflections reflect the variety of people I meet. Students, staff, friends, family, believers, non-believers, atheists, agnostics, not to mention the variety of faiths, beliefs, and non-beliefs. Most of those I meet want to understand life better so they can be happy and live well. If there is any common thread in these stories it is that they have all been shared in conversation with others when we were trying to make sense of things.

If anything, this publication is a testament to the time we spend with others and what we can harvest from these precious interactions. Our internet age is taking up a lot of our time and there is only so much of it. I seldom remember much of what is on screen, but I really remember the stories I shared with people and those they shared with me.

Most of the quotes were given to someone who needed to hang them on their fridge door. They needed to begin to think differently because the way they were thinking wasn't helping them.

When I pray, I often fumble though the events that led to these stories, and indeed others as well. It amazes me that God finds extraordinary ways to dip into our lives. If we've been strangers to the gentleness of God, or he has been a stranger to us, I hope we can dip into one another's presence this Lent with the assistance of these reflections.

Dedication

I wish to dedicate this book to all the students who have graced me with their presence and company over the last number of years in DIT. Their many and varied situations have encouraged me to dip more deeply into the mystery we call life. I am continually challenged but continually refreshed by their presence. I dedicate it also to the many staff who have an unbelievable ability to care and encourage way beyond what contracts and job descriptions dictate. They have inspired me to 'do more' and to 'be more'.

#a_pint

We were sitting over our pints talking. Two priests catching up. We were beyond the usual gossip and stuff that is talked about by priests. I was enjoying my pint as I had been off the drink for Lent.

'How did the (Easter) ceremonies go?' I asked. 'Grand', he said. 'What did you talk about at the Easter Mass?' 'Nothing much', he said, 'just the need to roll back a stone or two and let the light in.' I've never forgotten what he said.

The Christian of the future will be a mystic or he will not exist at all.

Karl Rahner SJ

. . . .

#being_heard

Prisons are strange places but people are still people, and often it is the prison itself that makes people behave in certain ways. On occasion, some prisoners are put on watch because the authorities are fearful that they might harm themselves. Once on watch they are visited by the chaplain and others.

I learned some things in those conversations. In order for real learning to take place one must have a question and the obvious one was 'why did you harm yourself, when you could have died?' Of course they never really had the answer but from our conversations, I figured there were basically two answers.

The first one was that they were tired of saying something important and urgent and not being heard, and the second was that they were trying to say something they couldn't understand well enough themselves to find the words to express it.

It is often in the privacy of the Sacrament of Confession where a person first gets to express their problems. Never mind what the priest hears; it is often their first time to hear how they feel about their situation. This, in itself, is healing.

When a person sits in front of me today with problems, I often wonder which of the two categories they fit into. When I preside over a funeral of a victim of a suicide, I often ask myself the same question.

Not being heard is no reason for silence.

Victor Hugo

. . . .

#caves

When Pope Francis was travelling to Cuba, a journalist on the flight asked him what the laity could do for the Church.

The question came from Noel Diaz, the son of a single mother who remembers when his mother could not afford to buy clothes for his First Communion. He is now a successful journalist in Los Angeles.

Pope Francis replied to Noel, 'Continue working . . . I need for you to get out of the caves'.

'Getting out of the cave' is a phrase used in Spanish to ask someone to leave a comfortable position in pursuit of something greater. This is a wholesome description of Lent; let's get out of our cave.

If you see anything mysterious or unusual
just enjoy it while you can.

Michael Leunig

· · · · · · · · ·

9

#change

While I was on a twelve week course on Family Therapy, the facilitator said one thing that has stayed with me forever – 'Most problems in families occur because a change has taken place that hasn't been negotiated properly'. People think that going off the drink is a reason for everyone to be happy but sobriety takes as much negotiation as drunkenness in a family setting.

Change is not only about excitement; it has its challenges. I remember a mother getting upset because her son who was in prison didn't want to see her. His reason was simple: he was due for release and visits were making him anxious. Everyone was talking about what they were going to do when he got out but he still had another hard few months to do. Other people's excitement was his chaos and upset. He just wanted to put the head down and do the time.

Most people, particularly in the Church, talk lovingly about change. Some, it appears, have an addiction to change. However, change that requires loss of status or necessitates more commitment is often avoided. We just want to put our head down and do our time as easily as possible. Change in places like parishes, schools or companies present an opportunity for some to advance their agendas and when that fails to happen they can slip back into their own rut, that is their own personal view of how the Church should be run. This is merely tinkering at the edges of our own comfort.

The journey of faith, especially for one on a Judaeo-Christian faith journey, is not simply one of change – it is one of transformation. Old ways are left behind and new ways are embraced. The ultimate expression of this is the Resurrection. The transformation that occurred in the person of Jesus allows our thinking on suffering and death to be transformed into ever greater possibilities. He just didn't tinker at the edges. The transformation of the Resurrection is so great that the story of the human condition can be re-written for those who believe and even for those who find it difficult to believe. Death is not mere change, it is radical transformation which is real and lasting change.

Death is the way into the divine presence,
the resolution of a lifetime of
wonder and waiting.

Sr Stan

· · · · · · · · · ·

#chaos

I've been involved, or even deeply immersed, in too many tragedies in my life. I don't seek them out. Events like the Berkeley balcony collapse when six J-1 students plunged to their death and others were injured leave a profound mark on one's soul. Many young people were deeply affected by this event as they saw their friends struggling with that thin line between life and death. Our thoughts and prayers continue to go out to those who suffer and to the families of those who died and who experienced life changing afflictions in this and other tragic events worldwide.

Words aren't adequate to fill the gap, only to say that there are times when things hit us so hard that the whole story of our life is utterly ripped apart and nothing makes sense anymore. The underlying narrative that once gave us meaning and hope can lie before us with little more power and energy than that of a spent battery. The challenge in the face of tragedy is to get to the core of things again, to separate what is important from what we have found not to be too important and build a new narrative that sustains us. This won't happen overnight and it often helps to chat things through with someone who won't judge us or mock us as we work things out. There are many who have faced this challenge in the past; this does not take away from the unique way in which we are affected by whatever we go through but they may be able to share some of their wisdom with us.

The worst scenario is not having a story to express who we are and what we do.

For the Christian, the season of Lent and Easter tells of a God who intervened in human history in an unimaginable way. He didn't come to a perfect time or a perfect place. In some sense, I'd love if he intervened in our times to show us how to deal with the challenges of the internet and social media! The one thing for sure though, is that he entered the chaos of people's lives and the chaos of our world.

Let us not be afraid of the chaos that is often around us and within us. In particular, let us not be afraid of the chaos we see in the lives of others: the homeless person, the refugee, the person who is recovering in hospital. If God entered our chaos let us not be afraid to step into the chaos of those we serve and love.

The world spins.
We stumble on.
It is enough.

Colum McCann, *Let the Great World Spin*

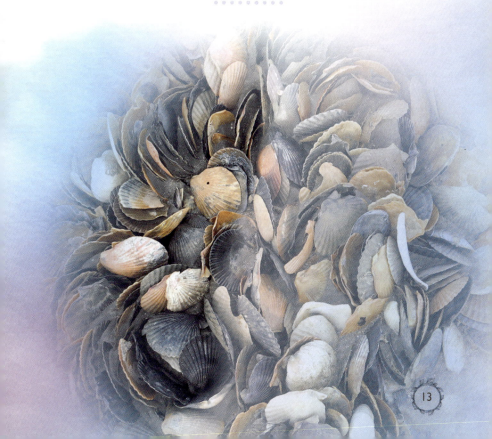

#cyberspace

In *Alone Together* Professor Sherry Turkle ponders the question 'why (do) we expect more from technology and less from each other?' One of Professor Turkle's most interesting findings concerns why we find technology so interesting and attractive. Seemingly the sound of a phone ringing, the sound of a text or the sound of an email alert lights up the same part of our brain as love does. In other words, it touches our deepest selves. It tells me that I am needed, I am wanted and that someone is thinking of me. This type of connection is only a substitute for real connection: we are fooling ourselves if we think that the sound of a text is one and the same thing as a genuine healthy human relationship. A text can't beat a good hug!

Electronic connection can distract from a space that ought to be filled with genuine human engagement. As Professor Turkle observes 'we are moving from conversation to connection'. The busy world of modern technology keeps us distracted from the world of interpersonal communication where we are real to one another, present to one another and supportive of one another.

I often see students in new situations standing awkwardly with hands raised and fingers sliding across screens to distract from the discomfort of loneliness or isolation. To be honest, I've done it myself. New technologies are creating their own anxieties rather than reducing them. Technology gives us the ability to communicate across space and time in a way that was unimaginable just a few decades ago. However, it cannot not tell us what to say! Now there's a source of anxiety if you need one.

Cyberspace cannot compensate for real space.
We benefit from chatting to people face to face.

Jonathan Sacks

. . . .

#death_in_a_laundry_basket

There has been a big increase in the number of civil weddings and secular funerals in Ireland these last few years. Having attended a funeral with no prayers, the father of a friend of mine who is a devoted Catholic said, 'I find it hard enough not saying prayers but (referring to the modern wicker coffin which he'd never seen before in Church or crematorium) I can't understand why they wanted to be buried in a laundry basket!'

One of the challenges facing a Church today is being able to say what is the value of a religious service. Following the referendum on same-sex marriage one person in conversation said to me that the Church failed to articulate the distinct aspects of sacramental marriage. This may be true but understanding the sacramental nature of anything takes more than one conversation.

Maybe our modern world has little space left to understand the mystical side of things. Maybe in a world of self-sufficiency there is little room for grace. At the time of St Bernard 'foot-washing', as outlined in the Gospel of John, was deemed to be a sacrament. Some of those responsible for leadership wanted 'foot-washing' to be a sacrament. John's Gospel, as you may be aware, substitutes the account of the Last Supper with a scene where Jesus washes the feet of his disciples. This is enacted in the Mass of the Lord's Supper every Holy Thursday.

To break through the apathy and resignation of today's world to things of faith, maybe one could consider making 'foot-washing' another sacrament to highlight the plight of those who are disenfranchised and who are our brothers and sisters in God. When fewer and fewer are seeing the value of sacramental institutions, maybe highlighting the sacramental value of our service to the world is more important than ever. The Church is often perceived as offering 'salvation from above' today. Foot washing, and the service of love to our brothers and sisters highlights the presence of 'salvation from below'.[1]

This is how the Good Samaritan acted. Jesus does not only exhort us; as the Fathers of the Church taught, he is hwimself the Good Shepherd who draws near to each person and "pours upon their wounds the oil of consolation and the wine of hope"

Portuguese Common Preface VIII, Pope Benedict, Fatima, 13 May 2010

. . . .

The most convincing sign that we are disciples of the Lord, and therefore the sign that attracts people most strongly to become his disciples, we can call the sacrament of fraternal love.

Olivier Quenardel

. . . .

---

[1] Ideas taken from a talk by the Cistercian monk, Br Olivier Quenardel, at an international Colloquium in 2015 at the Táize Community which I heard read by Br Martin at Lauds one morning in Glenstal Abbey.

#dementia

The funeral was taking place the next morning. It was a long day. As it went into the night I headed over to the house to prepare for the events of the following day. The phone calls had come at thirty minute intervals such was the anxiety about going to the funeral. The clothes had to be put out. 'Can't wear that – it doesn't go with the trousers'. Another half-hour of fashion consultancy and eventually I could head home.

The next morning meant an earlier start so that I could to get to the funeral with my parents. Earlier shower, earlier breakfast, earlier prayers, and so on. Before departing I phoned to check in. 'I'm coming down to bring you to the funeral' to which the reply was, 'what funeral?' You get used to it I suppose!

Trying to join the dots between what went on the night before with the following morning is the issue. When you don't try to join them there is no problem. How much of our lives are spent joining dots some of which can't be joined, some of which won't ever be joined and others that just demand too much if they are joined.

Sharing one's life with people who have various forms of memory loss is very challenging because their simple momentary conception challenges our complex construction of what we think ought to be. We have to learn to give it away so we can enter the moment of beauty that another holds before us.

I look forward to eternity if I am fortunate enough to be welcomed into it. It is one large dementia space where there is no pressure to join the past or the future or any of our 'complex constructions' to the present because the present is all that there is in eternity.

Let us act on what we have,
since we have not what we wish for.

Blessed John Henry Newman

· · · · · · · · ·

#detox

Did you ever do a detox? I did once and, to be honest, it did me the power of good. The detox was based on the assumption that the foods we crave are the ones that cause us most harm. The detox worked, I felt a lot better and I was a lot healthier afterwards. However, I never thought of prayer as detoxing! Read on ..

I once heard the theologian James Alison give an inspiring talk on prayer. What he said helped me. I had always imagined that the nature of Jesus was such that he'd get down to business immediately when it came to prayer. A direct line so to speak. Off he went into the desert and then, an immediate union with the Almighty.

Alison's theology is based largely on a theory of imitation; that is, we learn by imitating others. This is technically called mimetic desire (a technical term introduced by the French historian and psychologist René Girard). Mimetic desire involves the imitation of the desires of other people; we want what they want. The desires of some people are worth the effort but many others are destructive. Alison made the point that Jesus often went to the desert to detox from desires that had the potential to ruin him. We only have to look at the episode of the three temptations in Matthew's Gospel. In this episode, three narratives were put to him that could ultimately distract him from his core mission resulting in immediate gratification and long term discontent.

The first destructive narrative was the temptation to appease his hunger or satisfy his immediate human needs: the same way we'd be tempted to have another drink or cake; *ah go on, go on, go on!* Familiar words and a familiar situation for us all. The second temptation was to power, a power that'd take the sting out of life by breaking all the natural borders and boundaries that some of the elite and those with money or in a position of power succumb to today. Thirdly, the temptation was to have the old ego massaged. Sure we love it don't we – we can often turn the conversation around to how great we are! I remember someone commenting that your man is a self-made man and he worships his maker!

The point is that any narrative can take hold of us and destroy us. Maybe it's time to look on prayer or time out as a time to detox from the things that we can so often desire but which may have the potential to ruin us by distracting us from what is important.

When we have come to believe in the voices that call us worthless and unlovable, then success, popularity, and power are easily perceived as attractive solutions.
The real trap, however, is self-rejection. As soon as someone accuses me or criticizes me, as soon as I am rejected, left alone, or abandoned, I find myself thinking, "Well, that proves once again that I am a nobody." Self-rejection is the greatest enemy of the spiritual life because it contradicts the sacred voice that calls us the "Beloved." Being the Beloved constitutes the core truth of our existence.

Henri J.M. Nouwen

#divine_absence

The front pages of the newspapers and our online newsfeeds make the world appear as if it is falling apart. God seems to be more absent than present to the world. A person of faith may begin to wonder if God's wish for the world is mere fantasy.

There are days when I pray for God's intervention in the world. The selfish satisfaction would be immense if I could just look into the eyes of those who scoff and sneer and say 'told you so'. But God seems silent and I am not getting my way.

There are occasions, I admit, when God has broken through silence. When I visited Rwanda to hear the story of people of faith who survived the genocide, I heard lots of silence broken open. One religious sister who experienced horrendous brutality and personal suffering was inspiring. I asked the obvious question, 'how did you feel about God when all this murder and brutality was going on around you – should he have intervened to stop it?' She replied without even thinking as the answer was deep within her. 'I would not put blame for this on the shoulders of God'.

Ministry easily becomes a middle-class profession for clergy or a nights-and-weekend hobby for lay people.

Fr Emmanuel Katongole

#enemy

'Love your enemy' is easy for some people. There are those who cannot live without an enemy. They learn to feed off negativity. They can make others appear to be horrendous human beings who lack basic goodness. This creation is often a figment of their imagination but necessary to sustain their own warped sense self-worth and their drive. They love the presence of an enemy because without one, they'd have to consider their own heart and soul and this is too difficult for them. An enemy gives justification to a world view that distracts from personal well-being.

Jesus suffered under such people. He was made to be an enemy of the people to suit those in power. May we be protected from such people and the damage they do. The heart is too tender a space to be wasted on such negativity.

Jesus said, "Father, forgive them, for they do not know what they are doing." And they divided up his clothes by casting lots.

Luke 23:34

#environment

At the Parliament of World Religions in Melbourne there were some fascinating inputs. None were more intriguing than those from indigenous communities including Aboriginal people from Australia, Inuit, and North American Indians.

The civilisations of these communities are complex but their complexity veils a great deal of common sense that usually serves to protect and sustain them. They are remarkably good at this despite all the obstacles that the western and colonial world has thrown at them. The ability to protect and sustain a community into the future is a great challenge to many governments today. In fact one definition of social cohesion is the ability of a society to sustain and regenerate itself.

These indigenous communities are facing ever greater challenges to their way of life. Despite the belief by some that Global Warming and Climate Change are an exaggeration, one Inuit Eskimo related an interesting story. Every year they move their Caribou Deer to new feeding grounds. This tradition and path has been in place for thousands of years and is necessary for the survival of the deer and the people. For the first time ever in the memories and the stories of the people a tragedy befell them. While herding the Caribou across a frozen lake the ice cracked and most of the deer ended up in a watery grave. For the people, this was tragedy of immense proportion and remains a deep challenge to their way of life making sustainability near impossible.

Ulrich Beck has a term for the world we live in today. He created the term 'World Risk Society' underlining that never before in the history of the world have people the ability to destroy the earth. The 'risk' that the world can be destroyed by the actions of even one human being runs very high in today's world. The story from the Inuit man highlights this.

On the one hand, scriptures struggle to address this problem that confronts the world today. When they were written 'risk' did not run at the same levels. However, scripture has some important principles to guide us. Many of these are captured in Pope Francis's encyclical on the environment entitled *Laudato Si*.

> *These ancient stories (Old Testament), full of symbolism, bear witness to a conviction which we today share, that everything is interconnected, and that genuine care for our own lives and our relationships with nature is inseparable from fraternity, justice and faithfulness to others.*

Pope Francis, *Laudato Si*, par. 7

#frankenstein

I pretended I wasn't scared when I watched an old black and white Frankenstein movie but I certainly lost a few hours' sleep after watching one as a child. The plot was very simple: a crazed professor (Victor) was convinced he could create life. Both he and his loyal helper made their way to a graveyard to find a freshly buried corpse. A few adjustments to the remains in a remote castle, a good lightning storm and, hey presto, the dead come back to life. Never the prettiest figure as the enhancements that allowed the 'monster' come to life limited his appeal.

The story always had a heroine with whom the monster had an attraction and, like a teenager, he struggled with his feelings. During the second half of the movie things go pear-shaped. The monster becomes jealous of the love that the heroine has for another man who is easier on the eye than poor Frankenstein. His misplaced anger causes him to do silly things and fills the locals with terror until he is hunted down and destroyed. The only one who holds onto the possibility of humanity in this fearsome creature is the heroine of the story who brings a tear to the eye of the monster in his final hours.

With the passing of years, I see the Frankenstein story differently. When we look at the neglect of the environment and the fallout from neo-liberal market and even the day to day complexity of computerisation wherein one cannot allow for human situations, the moral of Frankenstein strikes a chord for me. The novel tells us that we create the monsters that destroy us and how true is this today?

Jesus had his own Frankenstein monsters. One day, when he went to the temple, he saw all the money changers and dealers destroying a sacred place. He lost it with them and set about throwing them out. There are days when I sit back and look at all the problems I am dealing with, and when I honestly ask how many of them are of our own making I can understand the frustration and anger of Jesus in the temple. It is so easy to blame the homeless for being homeless, the refugee for leaving his home and the drug abuser for abusing but this sometimes distracts from 'the monster' that created the problem in the first place.

There are many things that can only be seen through eyes that have cried.

Blessed Archbishop Oscar Romero

• • • • • • • • •

#goldfish

I'm looking at beautiful goldfish in a garden pond. Some are completely motionless, others seem to be dancing with the sunbeams that break into the water. They look quite content and at home. There's plenty to do it seems. I think of the goldfish I had as a child. I won it in a competition and had to find ways of 'storing' it until I got a proper goldfish bowl. Every day the poor creature looked out of the glass distracted by an odd visit skyward to feed off the seed like mixture that we called 'fish-food'. Compared to these creatures in the pond it's life was hellish!

Any talk of cruelty was eased by the understanding that the goldfish had a short memory, so they basically forget the limits of the environment within which they are expected to thrive. In people, loss of memory can cause anxiety and confusion that can be lived out in many strange ways: anger, despair and chaos. You see, remembering is not just about recall – it's about making things present. When you cannot make present the things that are important, even in your mind, life can begin to fall apart.

The aboriginal people use song and ritual to make the spirit of their ancestors present among them. This 're-membering' holds the people and the community together. They don't see groups as groups of individuals but as a communal collection who are bound to hold a story and memory in place. If the story goes – so do the people. Story therefore is not just about recall or 'having a laugh' it's about making deeper things present.

Sundays in churches are not just about recalling a historical event that took place two thousand years ago. They are about allowing this event to be as present today as it was then so we can live differently and live well. If we forget this story or fail to remember due to neglect or being too busy with other things, then this can cause anxiety and confusion that can be lived out in many strange ways with the accompanying anger, despair and chaos individually and communally that comes with memory loss.

When we suffer from amnesia,
every form of serious authority for faith is
in question, and we live unauthorised lives of
faith and practice unauthorised ministries.

Walter Brueggemann

#hurleys

One of most memorable childhood activities for me was travelling out to various ditches around the country to find ash trees suitable to make hurleys. No one doubts the magnificence and majesty of Ireland's great national sport. One sports commentator claims that the day of the All-Ireland Hurling Final should be declared a National Holiday such is the atmosphere and the following around the sport. However, the hurleys that beat the ball around the park have to come from somewhere.

Although they are all carved from ash trees, hurleys are made to different designs. The goal keeper's hurley can have a wider base to increase the chance of stopping a fast ball as it heads towards the goal mouth. Some counties have their own specific designs that have been passed on over the centuries. I was mystified as a young child watching one of Ireland's great hurley makers explain all these differences and subtleties.

Despite all these differences, hurley sticks carry one thing in common: they are all carved from ash trees that grow out of the side of a ditch. An ash tree that grows straight out of the ground is no good to the hurley maker. Every hurley has to have a spring in it; when it is pressed to the ground and pressure is placed on the hurley the player cannot afford to have it crack or split. The grain of the wood travels from the base of the hurley into the handle following the line of the tree growing out of the ditch and then turning its branches towards the sunlight. If the tree didn't have a bend in it then the hurley maker would only be wasting his time – the hurley wouldn't last too long into a game.

The Christian journey, when it moves beyond mere devotionalism and delves into the spiritual journey, can make little sense of straight lines. It is often the knarled knots and sweeping bends of our lives that reveal the face of God.

Let nothing perturb you.
Nothing frighten you.
All things pass.
God does not change.
Patience achieves everything.

St Teresa of Avila

#i'm_numb_therefore_I_am!

The age of the Enlightenment was characterised by the phrase of Descartes 'I think therefore I am'. We are in an age of the supremacy of the mind. But the mind is fighting back: depression, anxiety, suicide, break down, dementia, and Alzheimers all are symptoms of minds saying, enough, no more. In a reflection on what the internet is doing to our brain the author Nicholas Carr says,

what the(inter)net seems to be doing is chipping away at my capacity for concentration and contemplation. My mind now expects to take in information the way the net distributes it: in a swiftly moving stream of particles.

I don't know about you, but I used to be able to remember phone numbers, now I hardly remember my own. My brain is often numb with the amount of information I have to take in and ironically, as a result, I am less able to remember anything! Maybe the catch phrase for our time therefore is 'I'm numb therefore I am'.

There are a lot of advantages to our age but putting weight on one aspect of our humanity to the neglect of other important aspects of our being cannot be good for us. Though the mind and knowledge may be of great importance today, the soul and her accompanying wisdom are of more importance than ever. The two things that are being displaced more and more in daily life are conversation and contemplation: both are the doorways to wisdom. More often than not, to get the attention of another, and often our significant other, we have to distract them from their distractions.

We do not think ourselves into new ways of living, we live ourselves into new ways of thinking.

Richard Rohr

. . . .

#identity

I often wonder how St Patrick would describe himself. Did he see himself as a constant migrant? Did he come back to Ireland because he felt an affinity with the people? Was he just aware of the fluidity of the world of his time, prompted by trade and transport not unlike globalisation today? Did he feel constrained in his own place among his family and community? Was he just plain restless? Did his early experience of slavery discommode him? Was he someone who rose above tribal identity and found his identity in his work and his belief?

All these questions lead us to both wonder and understand how St Patrick is relevant to us today. For many years, religious faith in Ireland gave us a sense of belonging. Many identified themselves with the school they went to, the parish they attended or their college. Today, identity is changing because our world is changing. St Patrick is a good model for us in this age of globalisation and seemingly endless emphasis on nationalism and sovereignty. As someone who, we believe, lived in a number of places often against his will, his identity lay beyond what geographical borders dictate.

It was from his struggling heart that prayers like this took shape:

May the Strength of God guide us.
May the Power of God preserve us.
May the Wisdom of God instruct us.
May the Hand of God protect us.
May the Way of God direct us.
May the Shield of God defend us.
May the Angels of God guard us.
– Against the snares of the evil one.

May Christ be with us!
May Christ be before us!
May Christ be in us,
Christ be over all!

May Thy Grace, Lord,
Always be ours,
This day, O Lord, and forevermore.
Amen.

#image

Many years ago when we were told about the hazards of alcoholism in secondary school, we were given the image of a timid, shy person who had to consume alcohol to gain courage to socialise. Years later, I've come to understand the damage that is done to the person who has to hide behind addiction. The task of recovery involves meeting the person you felt was unworthy of attention and loving them back into wholeness and worthiness again.

Conversations with students have made me realise that the addictions today are more subtle. Students tell me that they are more and more under pressure to project an image of themselves that is socially acceptable and, like the alcoholic, they often find themselves suppressing their real self.

In this regard, one truth that students find revealing when I share it with them is the one that tells of the impact of modern devices. They are engendering a new narcissism that creates personalities that are more and more fragile. The insecurity of this fragility means that people are seeking more and more affirmation from shallow agents which can only prop us up until we need more from them.

It's hard for God to get a look in, as he is really only interested in the person that we are. Over and over again in the gospel, through his Son, the Father calls people from falsehood to truth. He's a lot easier on the real person who struggles: he finds oceans of forgiveness and understanding for them. It's the false people he can't work with. Let's get over creating the tacky image of ourselves that we create so we can be an acceptable 'image' to those who don't really matter. As my mother says, 'it's all very false son'. It's our deepest real and true selves that matters and it is this that is deeply loveable.

Our job is to love others without stopping to inquire whether or not they are worthy.

Thomas Merton

#impressionist

Sitting in front of a Monet painting of waterlilies is a profound experience. The delicate play of the light on the pond makes everything dance. The senses are struggling to focus until one spot is found through which we feel a part of the scene. No longer an observer, I become an active participant in this cacophony of colour.

Impressionists have given themselves permission to see things as they appear to themselves and not necessarily as to how another person would perceive the objects in view. We have a long history in Europe of the concept of a deity being held in place by an authority that presents an image without question. Dogma has little time for impressionists. For the more rigid, perception is what you are told to perceive rather than how you may actually perceive things.

But time moves on. Our world is much more individualised and personalised. As a result, belief seems to be shying away from historical certainty and is giving way to future diversity. This has not gone unnoticed by the European sociologist Ulrick Beck. He records that people are moving from a concept of God our Father to one where people are now a father to their own god. Be this good or bad or right or wrong does not seem to matter as this is just the way things are.

Most religious traditions are founded around an image of a leader sharing wisdom with a group of followers. Jesus sat and spoke to the crowds on the mountain-side, Buddha spoke under the lotus tree to his monks, in Islam the *Qur'an* (recitation) is so named because believers learned it by listening to public readings and recitations. The aborigines in Australia gather as a community around the fire to share their stories and beliefs. Spirituality may seek individual paths but real faith requires a community that has a history.

The purpose of faith is to bring us closer to the mystery of the eternal and to make the world a better place for the most part. For Christians, the belief is that this mystery is encapsulated by the word 'love'. As I explore my own 'impressionist' view of the world, the key observation is whether my god has me wallowing in self-love or immersing myself in the love of others. Alternatively, I could start by asking myself does the god I have created hate the same people I hate; if so, maybe my image of god is created in my own image rather than in his!

I'm very fond of Jesus Christ.
He may be the most beautiful guy who walked the face of this earth. Any guy who says "Blessed are the poor. Blessed are the meek" has got to be a figure of unparalleled generosity and insight and madness ... A man who declared himself to stand among the thieves, the prostitutes and the homeless. His position cannot be comprehended. It is an inhuman generosity. A generosity that would overthrow the world if it was embraced because nothing would weather that compassion.

Leonard Cohen

#inri

It was the last week before the much needed Easter holidays. It was a particularly late Easter so we were all exhausted. Last day before the break, what better way to conduct a religion class than read the biblical account of Easter. They loved the drama, the characters and the plot. A few questions here and there but generally they hung onto the story.

One question came from the fella in the front bench, 'Sir, what does INRI mean?'. Rather than answering, I put the question out to the rest of the class. I didn't have to wait long, a few hands shot up. One hand surprised me; he didn't put the hand up too often! I decided to go around the room. First answer, 'Emmmmm, I forget'. Next answer, 'something about a King'. 'Very good, close, but a little but more is needed', I replied with all the necessary positive affirmation. Finally, I turned to the surprising candidate, 'Yes Mark, what does INRI stand for'. Without flinching, and delighted at being asked, enthusiastic to share his knowledge, he blurted out, 'I'm Nailed Right In – sir'.

I had to excuse myself and told them to write down a few paragraphs from the passage we were reading. I went to the staff room unable to talk I was so convulsed with laughter. When I eventually settled, I shared my new found knowledge with my colleague Con who became equally convulsed.

That was a few years go now. Just a few months back, Con passed away after a long battle with cancer. Like most funny stories, there is a nub of truth. Certainly, for Con and for many others, we can find ourselves nailed to the cross of suffering and try as we might, there is little to make us laugh. There are moments when we can give thanks for what has been, and live with the hope and anticipatory joy of what is to come. I look forward to sharing laughter with Con and many others once again.

In the Baroque period the liturgy used to
include the 'Risus Paschalis', the Easter
laughter. The Easter homily had to contain
a story that made people laugh, so that the
church resounded with a joyful laughter.
That may be a somewhat superficial form
of Christian joy. But is there not something
very beautiful and appropriate about laughter
becoming a liturgical symbol? And is it not a
tonic when we still hear, in the play of cherub
and ornament in Baroque churches,
that laughter which testified to the
freedom of the redeemed?

Pope Benedict XVI

#lent_is_often_not_ours_to_choose

Choosing Lent can be an act of luxury. Deciding to do something or to give up something on Ash Wednesday every year can be phenomenally privileged. A few years ago, I visited Rwanda to meet many people who lived through the genocide. In 1994 they had no power over when Lent began. In actual fact, Lent started on Easter Thursday precisely at the time when it should have drawn to a close. Following the downing of an aircraft with the President on board there was widespread slaughter of one group of people by another. It was merciless, and when it was going on it appeared that there was no hope ever of an Easter as those who saw immense suffering and death felt that the country had descended into hell.

One lady I met told the story of her Lent which has left an indelible mark on her life. Her fiancée found his way to relative safety within the confines of the *Hôtel Des Milles Collines* which was a protectorate of the United Nations. The plight of those in the hotel was portrayed in the movie *Hotel Rwanda*. He heard that his future wife was in danger and, against the best advice, he left the hotel to find her. He then brought her from her home back to the hotel. The journey of those few short miles was miraculous. Christine spent forty days in the hotel before their release was negotiated. She told us that Lent has never been the same again as she remembers those forty days and nights when life was very fragile and death tormented every sinew of their being.

I was there the night that they went back to the room that they stayed in for their forty days. During the genocide there was very little food, very little room and often the only water they had to drink was that which was left in the swimming pool. Every room was packed to capacity and everyone was fraught.

Those forty days changed the pattern of their living. How they love, how they live, how they pray and how they understand the precious gift of life that was rewritten and recast on their hearts. The forty days of Lent can fall unexpectedly on us but we live in the hope of an Easter even when it cannot be glimpsed or even imagined. To choose Lent is luxury at times, but there are occasions when Lent is not ours to choose but neither then is Easter. To embrace Easter is to live differently.

Let Him Easter in us.

Gerard Manley Hopkins

· · · · · · · · ·

#lent_should_be_all_year_round

A friend of mine from the Lutheran tradition has a very interesting question about Catholic Lent. 'Why do you need to do these things once a year – why don't you do all these good things all year?' I must say I had no answer.

When you cut to the quick, there is no doubt that for a Christian the entire year should be Lenten in spirit but we are frail people and we need a good kick in the backside every so often, and an opportunity to benefit from that self-same kick. In fact, many of the great spiritual writers would hold the view that we should have a Lenten mind-set all year round.

Some of these same writers would point out that Lent falls at a time of year when the pantry is running low. This was particularly true prior to the invention of freezers and modern transport. When the pantry was all you had, there was a sense of 'making do' until spring time produced fresh produce. Lent helped this process. Rather than Lent being an occasion to make a personal decision to give something up it was a chance to live with the reality that the resources of the earth are scarce, and that we live in a fragile world where we have to be respectful of these realties.

The goal of fasting is inner unity. This means hearing, but not with the ear; hearing, but not with the understanding; it is hearing with the spirit, with your whole being. The hearing that is only in the ears is one thing. The hearing of the understanding is another, but the hearing of the spirit is not limited to any one faculty, to the ear, or to the mind. Hence, it demands the emptiness of the faculties, and when the faculties are empty, then your whole being listens ... Fasting of the heart empties the faculties, frees you from limitations and from preoccupations.

Thomas Merton

#mindfulness

I wonder about mindfulness. It's the 'in thing' at the moment. Everybody is being mindful; well at least they've done the course, be it for half a day or for three months in an Ashram.

They know how to body scan: to take off their shoes and feel the ground beneath; to check in on various parts of the anatomy, especially those places that are tense. And sure, if sitting down is not mindful enough, you can go on a mindful walk and even do a bit of mindful eating – never in front of the television though!

In truth, it is a wonderful science. As one who has struggled to pray and mediate in a Benedictine or Jesuit setting, I wonder what all the fuss is about. Isn't it just an occasion to sit still and let the body catch up with the soul or the mind depending on your framework of belief?

There are a few things I have come to understand a little better about mindfulness. First of all, it is not a course; it is a practice, something that is done every day to develop an outlook and a way of being. Secondly, it hasn't fallen off the trees. In many ways, it has been around for a long time in monasteries. From a Buddhist point of view, it is part of the process whereby one can become detached from what is destructive or unimportant or, from a Christian point of view, to become attached to whom or what is important. Thirdly, it has an ultimate outcome which is compassion. To start with self-compassion and move into compassion for others is the true ideal. As one of the great practitioners, Sharon Salzburg reminds us, 'Loving-kindness and compassion are the basis for wise, powerful, sometimes gentle and sometimes fierce actions that can really make a difference – in our lives and those of others'.

Mindfulness helps me greatly. It helps me get on the road towards what matters. However, I nearly always find myself coming back to a line from which compassion oozes – when Jesus met

the rich young man, he realised that the young man had a lot to learn and so the gospel tells us that 'Jesus looked steadily at him and loved him' *(Mk.10:21)*.

Sabbath, in the first instance, is not about worship. It is about work stoppage. It is about withdrawal from the anxiety system of Pharaoh, the refusal to let one's life be defined by production and consumption and the endless pursuit of private well-being.

Walter Brueggemann

. . . .

#moving_on

Having walked a road with many people in various situations, I note that in a new environment people can have two reactions. They can either explode or implode . . . let me explain. Sometimes new environments give a person an opportunity to achieve new objectives, to reach for new horizons. This new environment makes a person realise new possibilities, even a greater sense of being alive. On the other hand, a person in a new setting can find that the new challenges make them feel inadequate, always struggling to achieve, finding things more difficult, even simple things.

Whether it be moving to a new neighbourhood, going to college or heading to a new land these things can bring out one or both of these reactions. Some things give us a sense of excitement, other things can find us struggling. Both reactions have advantages and disadvantages. Both are indications that we are doing something new. Changed environment affects us – if it didn't there'd be something wrong. Don't be overcome by either extreme, at least not for too long.

I wonder when Jesus arrived in Jerusalem whether he thought he had exploded or imploded?

The way you look at things is the most powerful force in shaping your life.

John O'Donohue

#never_prepared

Tony Bates is the founder of Headstrong. It is an organisation that promotes positive mental health among young people. I once had him sit with a group of people who were facing a very difficult situation. They were in the midst of the most horrendous tragedy; their worlds were falling apart. He discussed their situation in a very open, honest and one might say raw manner. He alluded to aspects of the situation that anyone else would have ducked and dived. I'll never forget one thing he said, 'You haven't prepared your children for this' the parents looked rather shocked, nearly angry with him. He then went on to say that 'neither are you prepared for this' at which they then looked absolutely confused. He then concluded with the words, 'neither should you be!'

They instantly got his point. We cannot spend our lives thinking that every bus we see has the potential to knock us down, that every car the ability to mount the pavement and impact us or every concert has the potential for a bombing. If this was the case, and if we adopted this attitude, our lives would go unlived. Of course we have to exercise caution and be diligent, but we have to embrace the gift we call life and try to live it to the full. Indeed, the Christian community remembers that every child is anointed on his or her heart at Baptism, asking that they will have the strength to withstand evil and dwell in goodness.

Acts of destruction are never impersonal,
abstract or merely material.
They always have a face,
a concrete story, names.

Pope Francis

#one_of_our_own

These are the words of city-centre Dublin people. They may be used to describe a Garda, a priest, the community nurse or a local bank manager. They are usually heard within earshot of the person they are directed at. It is an individual's, or a community's, way of saying that they accept you. I remember during my first week in a city parish, I shared a few moments in conversation with some local women. Just as I left them, and thinking I had impressed them with my competence, I overheard one of them say, 'Ah God love him, he's only a chiseller.'[2] Maybe I was meant to hear these words! A way of saying 'he's one of our own'.

When I look at statues or portraits of Saint Patrick, I often think he has truly been made 'one of our own'. Green clothing, clutching a shamrock with maps of Ireland etched in the background; he truly is one of us. Our hearts swell with pride when we walk the cities of the world and find cathedrals named in his honour: 'one of our own', and look at his impact.

Saint Patrick is so emblazoned with symbols of his Irishness that we forget he was an immigrant to Ireland. Not unlike the Holy Family and many families today, he was an undocumented migrant, a refugee, a slave, a member of a diaspora and a returnee. Yet somehow, he transcended all of these categories and made himself 'one of us'.

> *Your enemy is not the refugee;*
> *your enemy is the one who*
> *made them a refugee.*
>
> Tariq Ramadan

---

[2] Dublin slang meaning 'child'.

#orphans

A person of faith today may feel like they have been orphaned. In our particular circumstances of ill-health or loneliness we may feel totally abandoned by God. In our society we may, more and more, feel in a beleaguered minority as anything or anybody associated with Church is seen as a hurdle or barrier to a mature and vibrant society. Among some, the Church has become relegated to an opposition party's election slogan . . . 'if we get rid of them . . . all will be well'. These circumstances may have us feeling abandoned. In spite of this, Jesus says it is not necessary to feel like this. A man I knew lived until he was ninety-three. He achieved the highest that anyone could achieve in the world of business and society and yet he was orphaned at a very young age. He never attended school yet, as I say, he surpassed himself. We can be an orphan because that is the way the world describes us, but we are more than how others describe us.

The writer and mystic Thomas Merton, a Cistercian monk who lived in a monastery in Kentucky in the United States in the sixties said, 'how do you expect to arrive at the end of your own journey if you take the road to another's city? How do you expect to reach your own perfection by leading somebody else's life?' He goes on to say that, 'it takes heroic humility to be yourself and to be nobody but the person, or the artist, that God intended you to be'.

The man I knew who lived until he was ninty-three was orphaned, yet in his own mind, and in the mind of the God who created him, he refused to be defined by that. With 'heroic humility', he remained the person that, he felt, God intended him to be. For every one of us the challenge and the task is plainly put before us. God's Spirit helps us reach higher, harder and deeper in the belief that God's help is close as we strive to live an authentic, humane and contented life where we can be faithful to the journey that God wants for us, and not to become a prisoner in another's city.

It takes heroic humility to be yourself and to be nobody but the person, or the artist, that God intended you to be.

Thomas Merton

· · · · · · · · ·

#reality

I was speaking with a colleague during the week who is involved in manufacturing engineering. He told me of a group of students who set about to design a bicycle which, according to them, was going to change the world of cycling. It was to be the latest and best as they were using technology that people of previous generations would not have had access to. They sat at the computer for weeks, examining every detail and developing their revolutionary design.

One thing they did was to increase the size of the pedal and the size of the crank shaft between the foot-pedal and the bar that holds the two pedals together. The extra length and size, they said, would increase the torque allowing the cyclist exert more pressure on the pedal, thus enabling the bicycle to travel at a faster speed with less pressure and stress on the cyclist.

Eventually, the design was agreed on and they set about making the prototype. They were so confident of their design that they left little time for building the bike and testing a working model. When the final days arrived they conducted a test. It was all going well until every time the bike had to take a corner the pedal was so long that it hit the ground and the cyclist was thrown off the bike. My colleague was explaining that in days gone by you always started designing with a model, not the computer. A model would have exposed this problem earlier and they would have been able to adjust their design accordingly. Just because it looks good on a computer screen doesn't mean that it will work well in reality.

People can talk about religion over lattes and prosecco for long periods, but religion is something that must be lived. As Pope Francis told priests, 'they must know the smell of their sheep!' You can't realise that objective on a computer screen.

*An ounce of practice is worth more
than tons of preaching.*

Mahatma Gandhi

· · · · · · · · ·

#shifting_sands

As the plane descends into Dublin towards the westerly runway, Howth Head comes plainly into view if you are sitting on the left hand side of the plane. Immediately, one spots a spur of sand known to locals as *The Bull Wall, Dollier* or *Dollymount*. The lighthouse out in the middle of the bay is called *Poolbeg* or *An Pól Beag* in Gaelic. The direct translation means, *The Little Hole*. The story goes that ships were unable to make it up the Liffey due to a large sand-bar across its mouth and they anchored safely in the Little Hole. The locals made a trade of racing out to the ships to take the goods to shore on their small rowing boats – first out got the work. The small boats are called 'skiffs' and they race on the river to this day.

In 1715, in an attempt to reclaim land for the City of Dublin, Captain Blythe of *Mutiny of the Bounty* fame set about building a wall out to the Poolbeg Lighthouse. The cumulative effect of the wall was an increase in the force of the water leaving the Liffey as it travelled a narrower channel. It wasn't part of the plan but because of the flow of the water, the sand bar across the bay shifted and the stretch of sand now known as *Dollier* was formed. Basically the sandy silt was lifted by the water which was flowing faster and stronger as a result of the new wall. The silt from the sand bar was transported in a westerly direction where it found a new home.

There are things in life that can prove to be major blocks and obstacles, maybe patterns of our own behaviour or the behaviour of others that can impede human flourishing. Institutions we are aligned with can be more interested in self-preservation than the promotion of their core mission. It can appear that the ships of opportunity remain outside the harbour of possibility. Lent is an occasion to shift some sandbars that are impeding me from living a more wholesome life with God. It may be about doing or not doing, about giving up or not giving up but please allow his grace to carve a channel through our intentions and our actions.

I do not at all understand the mystery of grace only that it meets us where we are but does not leave us where it found us.

Anne Lamott

#skies

I'll never forget him. He was in the psychiatric hospital in Sydney, forlorn, forgotten and confused. It was a bright day outside. The sky was its normal blue with the usual golden medallion suspended above us, its persistent heat reminding us of its presence. You come to expect it in Australia, unlike Ireland of course.

The phone call alerting me to this young man's predicament carried the near predictable words, 'we thought the change would do him good!' I have learned a lot about travel and migration in my life. It is best summed up in the words of a man I knew who was a long-time member of Alcoholics Anonymous. He said, 'sure the first person you meet getting off the plane is yourself!' Oh how right he was. The young man in hospital, and his family, thought with the sunshine and the general good weather he wouldn't need his medications.

Some people move to find a new beginning, and it works, but you start with the same raw material and a little bit of wisdom picked up on the path of life. Maybe a holiday gives us a well-earned break, an occasion to shake off tiredness and approach life with a new vigour but we are essentially the same person. If we really want to change it's the journey inwards which Lent encourages that matters. This journey is infinitely more important and rewarding than the journey over land and sea.

Christ of the mysteries,
I trust You to be stronger than
each storm within me.

Extract from the sixth century prayer of St Brendan the Navigator

. . . .

#survival_of_the?

At a recent seminar, the speaker told us that we are all focused on 'survival' these days. This is our unconscious default position. The clamour of life is such that more and more people wonder how they will make it through the day. I can only imagine what it is like for someone who leaves a homeless shelter in the morning wondering how he or she is going to survive and make it through the day. Furthermore, I often wonder what it must be like for a migrant to put a foot into the Sahara hoping they have enough food and water for the journey. For many, survival is the default position and not just for those on the margins.

The seminar highlighted this but said 'well-being' should be our default position. To exist only to survive is demeaning to our human and even our divine task. The advance of economics, wealth and consumerism has actually displaced the time old task of 'well-being' with 'survival'.

One of the things about the hunter gatherer model is that while some were delegated with the task of survival for the community, others were delegated to look after the community. This wasn't as a result a strategic plan or a therapeutic intervention but simply because it was part of the natural order. In our age, the clear majority of people are living with survival as their default position. So wake up tomorrow with an eye on living well rather than mere survival. One of my favourite sociologists Zygmunt Bauman said, 'Why do I write books? Why do I think? Why should I be passionate? Because things could be different, they could be made better.'

There are other ways of finding satisfaction,
recipes for human happiness, enjoyment,
dignified and meaningful, gratifying life, than
increased consumption that
increases production.

Zygmunt Bauman

#tea

Ireland was renowned for years for 'visits'. It was not uncommon to arrive home from school to find a neighbour in the house having the chat and then dinner would be served around them . . . they might even share what was on offer. God knows why they needed to be there, most likely the 'chat' was about some issue that wasn't going away but the tea and company helped bid it adieu.

Tommy Tiernan has a funny sketch when he talks about the last World War. When Europe was being blown apart Ireland, he reminds us, was undergoing 'an emergency'. What was that emergency he observes? 'We had no tea'! Today, people might sign up for counselling or get medication for the type of thing the cup of tea sorted in times past! These visits were simple transfigurations; moments of revelation that made a difference and brought about a necessary change.

Our culture is shifting and changing so much that it is time to name what is being lost. We do not yet have the solutions to these questions, but the awareness that we live in an endangered world is present in more and more life situations.

Ulrich Beck

· · · · · · · · · ·

#the_county_jersey

This time of the year sees the ending of the leagues in the GAA and talk of the Championship. When August and September appear people start hustling for tickets, and even for flights to get home from abroad to watch their home county play in Croke Park. There is no other game in the world that creates so much excitement, and where the national and the local have such a unique synergy.

When I worked in Sydney I watched with bemusement the many Irish people who walked up Bondi Road with the county jerseys proudly on display. It's as if their sense of anonymity in this new place gives an extra push towards a recognition of identity; it's a way of saying 'I belong' when you feel lost.

Whenever I baptise a child, and I speak about dignity and identity, I know how hard it is to hold onto these simple words in life. When I pour water over the child's head my heartfelt prayer is that this child will always feel that they belong and are welcome at the well we call life.

I would love to live like a river flows,
carried by the surprise of its own unfolding.

John O'Donohue

. . . .

#the_devil

When I was teaching we used to say that if you knew the nickname the pupils had for you, you were very lucky. If you didn't know what your nickname was you'd have to be worried. They didn't want you to know! Nicknames are part of the culture of Dublin. One nickname that caused me concern was 'the Devil'. All sorts of things went round in my mind until I discovered that this person's family had a tradition of stoking the boiler in a local factory.

Another man, a bus conductor, was known simply as 'Pockets' because he used to eat his lunch from the pockets of his bus man's uniform. These nicknames accentuated a characteristic of these people or made reference to habits in their lives that, at times, they themselves hadn't even noticed.

Nicknames also fulfilled an important role. If an area had a particularly high number of people who carried the same surname, which often happened in rural parts of Ireland, people's nicknames were the only way of identifying exactly who you were talking about. 'Two-storey Murphy' was not necessarily someone who was good at story telling but a family who owned the only two-storey house in the area. If you were making a delivery to an area the first question you'd be asked is 'what Murphy would that be?' Nicknames can often help us to figure out who we are looking for and help us to find them. They also help us learn something about a person or a family.

The scriptures are littered with nicknames. God is often named as an eagle who shelters us under his wings. In Isaiah 66, God is a mother who gives comfort to her children. One of the most tangible names of God presented to us is in Psalm 23, when God is presented as a shepherd who looks after his sheep and leads them to fresh pastures and clear, safe waters.

All these names give the human mind a door onto the nature of God. No one captures everything so seeing a person as the sum total of their nickname would be to do them an offence. However, the one that constantly blows my mind is the one Jesus gave us. Simply put: God is our Father, Daddy, Abba. Jesus used this name to teach us a prayer which is still with us today. A wise person once said to me, when I was finding it difficult to pray, just use the first two words of the Lord's Prayer. They said that there was enough in those two words – *'Our Father'* – to teach us about the entire mystery of faith! It certainly helped me find my way.

In Jesus this expression 'Our Father' has no trace of routine or mere repetition. On the contrary, it contains a sense of life, of experience, of authenticity. With these two words, 'Our Father', He knew how to live praying and to pray living. Jesus invites us to do the same.

Pope Francis

· · · · · · · · ·

#the_mundane

When you visit a monastery for the first time you can be left in awe of the life of the monastic community: the beautiful chanting, the seemingly unprompted and admirable order; the mindful way, the quiet and encouraging environment, the good food and the cheerful disposition of the monks.

First impressions can be deceptive, however. I am sure that the monks find much of what I experience as 'wonder-filled' to be quite mundane! A regular schedule telling you that this is the way things will be for the rest of your life. A vow of stability which means that, even if you find someone particularly difficult or abrasive, you are stuck with them for the rest of your or indeed their earthly life. The office[3] which on initial hearing can be melodious and engaging can, I'm sure, be cumbersome and littered with distraction for the monk for whom it is a daily part of life.

This, however, is the life they have chosen. The belief is that if you are faithful to something or someone it will be faithful to you. For the monk, the project of life is not limited merely to earthly time but a place that is beyond time, namely eternity. This is less and less the contextualisation for life today.

The choice before us today is between the observation of a routine that helps us drill down into life and, with patient observation and dedication, find tremendous wealth and insight there; a wealth and insight that contextualises our lives, and sticking with the senses. If we stick with the senses we are eternally distracted, seeking the next buzz or new experience or to adopt the latest socially acceptable norm. In short, life can be eternity of distractions or a direction towards things eternal.

---

[3] The office refers to the prayers that are read by the monks a number of times during the day

When setting out on a journey,
never seek advice from those
who have never left home.

Rumi

· · · · · · · · ·

#the_prodigal_and_the_mother

He was dead for quite a while and she spoke about him a lot. Every conversation about him seemed unfinished; something ran deep that was unsaid. Eventually it came out. Her son had lived a colourful life. He had travelled the world before a strange hereditary disease took him from her. She missed him, but more than missing him, she wondered where he was in a deeply metaphysical sense. I had spoken with her a few times but, on this occasion, I felt compelled to push things a bit.

'Are you worried about him?' In true Irish style she didn't answer the question directly. 'I'd say he lived life to the full when he was alive' she said. 'Tell me' I asked, 'when did the father forgive the Prodigal Son?' She looked at me and rebuked me a bit, 'I'm no theologian', she said. 'I don't know about that!' I replied, 'but you're a mother and that certainly helps'. I continued, 'Go on then, when did he forgive him?'

'When he saw him coming towards the house?' 'Try again' I said. 'When he said sorry?' 'Maybe – try again'. 'When he hugged him?' and then she said sternly ... 'and that's my final answer'. She looked at me, 'and what's your answer smarty-pants?'. 'I don't think he ever forgave him!' Well, talk about a livid look! 'What do you mean she asked?' She stuttered and stammered, protesting and pontificating like mad. She couldn't get her head around what I was saying. Eventually she fell silent through sheer frustration, even anger.

'I don't think he ever forgave him because, well because he never needed to.' I added, 'I don't think he ever condemned him in the first place.' Her silence went deeper and she sat up carrying a peace that seemed to catch her unexpectedly. She knew immediately what I meant.

In truth, I don't know if I'm right or wrong on this one. I only know that when you peel back the idea of God's mercy in the stories and actions of Jesus, we are told that his mercy is richer and deeper than any human concept of mercy and forgiveness.

We come to love not by finding a perfect person, but by learning to see an imperfect person perfectly.

Sam Keen

• • • • • • • • •

#scales_of_tears

I am reminded of the story of a child asking daddy 'What is that thing that mammy stands on in the bathroom?' Daddy wondered for a moment and said, 'Oh, that's the bathroom scales darling.' 'Thanks daddy', said the child. After a moment she went on, 'Why does it make mammy say bold words?'

When we put ourselves onto health and fitness programs we put ourselves under pressure to perform to certain expectations. We expect things to change overnight and we get frustrated and angst-ridden if they don't; if the change doesn't measure up to our expectations.

Without creating a strategic plan, it's a good thing to ask ourselves at the beginning of Lent or at the start of a pilgrimage or Camino 'what are truly trying to gain for ourselves on this journey?' Sometimes it just needs to be put out there without a plan. One of the greatest contributions to the twentieth century was the twelve-step program. The first step is powerful beyond words; 'I am powerless over this situation and I hand it over to a power greater than myself.' That's enough to begin Lent or any journey with.

Aspire not to have more but to be more.

Blessed Archbishop Oscar Romero

. . . .

#tunes

The session was in full swing. Uileann pipes, fiddles, flutes and a myriad of other instruments. The assembled musicians numbered among the finest Irish traditional musicians in the world. A mother and her daughter were eating casual lunch while listening to the tunes. You can pack a lot of different tunes into a few hours. They paid their bill and, before they set off, one of them turned to me. 'They seem very good, we've really enjoyed the music,' she paused, 'but tell me is that the only tune they know?'

To the casual outsider Irish tunes can all sound the same. The intonation, source, name, style and category is lost on them. The blood, sweat and tears of the person who put a tune together and the moment that inspired it is not even up for consideration. There are many stories about tunes that'd fill pages. I love the one told by James Keane. Born in Dublin, he has lived most of his life in New York. He is an inspiring accordion player and boy can he tell stories about tunes! As a young man, he and his brother Sean made their way into the Fr Matthew Hall in Dublin, the home of *Fleadhs* and sessions in days gone by. As evenings at the Fr Matthew Hall drew to a close they were always tempted to stay on to hear tunes played by some of the great musicians of Ireland and on many occasions, because of this, had to walk home having missed the bus. That's the experience Keane thinks of when he plays the tune *Last Bus to Driminagh*. I often wonder did he write that tune while sitting on the pavement at God knows what hour of the morning wondering how he was going to get home ... again!

Every tune has a story but sometimes they can all sound the same. This is no different to people. We can all be herded into the one category and lose our individual traits. Every human being is created unique. That uniqueness goes beyond the fingerprint and retina identification. There is something unique in our soul that mirrors the divine purpose. Take time today to spot it in people you meet; even study it in yourself.

I don't know who — or what — put the question, I don't know when it was put. I don't even remember answering. But at some moment I did answer Yes to Someone — or Something — and from that hour I was certain that existence is meaningful and that, therefore, my life, in self-surrender, had a goal.

Dag Hammarskjöld

. . . .

73

#upside_down_leadership

I met a Native American at a conference once. He was a very happy, wholesome man, who carried a burden of belief about the way the world should be. The story of his people is troubled as one can only imagine. On many occasions in the past, they were in the way of colonial progress and today, they are often in the way of economic progress but, sadly, the larger powers seem to win out. I'd love to have spent more time with him and listen to his story but time caught up on us.

He had leadership potential and he knew it. His people had a chief but the day would come when he'd be the leader of his people. It was inevitable as he knew their hearts and he knew the value of the way of his ancestors and those living today.

I asked him if he looked forward to being the chief. He said, 'not really'. 'Why?' I asked. 'Well', he replied, 'I will own nothing.' I was a little confused, leadership in my political culture meant security, prestige and to a certain degree a position that is rewarded with wealth.

He went on to explain, 'If I am a chief and I see a person in my tribe who is cold and has no coat then I have to give them the coat I am wearing. I own nothing; what I have is for my people.' Which model, his one or the one that came to my mind, is the upside-down one or even better, which one is the right way up?

Do not wait for leaders,
do it alone,
person to person.

Saint Mother Teresa

. . . .

#violence

What is the opposite of violence? Peace, ceasefire, love, truce – the list could go on. The best answer I ever came across was that the opposite to violence is 'wonder and awe'. To be honest, when I first read this I was a tad dismissive but then I thought about it.

To carry out an intentional act of violence against a person, you need to see an aspect of that person that you can despise: it makes the violent act easier to commit. The idea of the Officer's Mess in the army is that the officer will have certain emotional distance from the foot soldier making it easier to give the command to approach enemy lines. And this is for their own soldiers; what must the perceptions of the enemy be?

To see a uniform, skin colour, class, religion or politics to the neglect of the person who bears these characteristics makes it easier to commit a violent action against them. Seeing the beauty of another and holding on to that beauty and uniqueness with a sense of wonder and awe makes it infinitely more difficult to commit an act of violence. Furthermore, to hold onto the magnificence of one's own being with a sense of wonder and awe greatly reduces the risk of doing violence to oneself.

Maybe it is no accident that 'wonder and awe' is a gift of the Holy Spirit. The first novena that ever took place was the time spent by the followers of Jesus between Easter and Pentecost waiting for something to happen. This year pray for this gift between Easter and Pentecost and pray that today's humanity will come to hold their brothers and sisters with a sense of 'wonder and awe' thus banishing violence.

There is no dichotomy between man and God's image. Whoever tortures a human being, whoever abuses a human being, whoever outrages a human being, abuses God's image.

Blessed Archbishop Oscar Romero

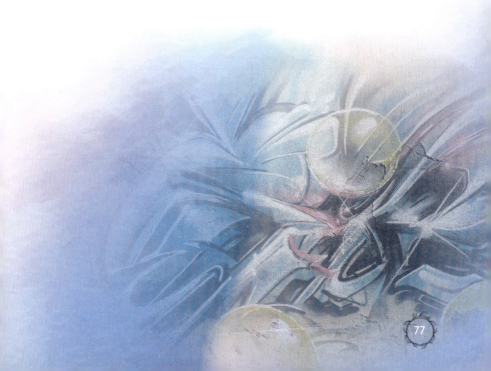

#where_will_it_all_end_up?

'Where will it all end up?' A question often posed today by people who value the role of the Church in their lives, their community and their society. To say that there is a lot of confusion tending towards despair about the future of the Church in Ireland and indeed Europe is commonplace.

The future lies more in creating great human beings and less about great institutions. Those who have made it to the top of the ecclesiastical structure were often people who made the institutions look great and their humanness was often not a priority. In a world that has enormous possibilities and increasingly diverse influences Christianity is desperate for more ambassadors and less bureaucrats.

The gospels remind us that people want to meet other people whose humanity points towards something worth striving for. 'All spoke well of him, how can this be they asked, "isn't this Joseph's son?"' *(Lk.4:22)*. 'And they were amazed, and asked, "what kind of man is this?"' *(Mt.8:28)*. 'The centurion, seeing what had happened, praised God and said, "Surely this was a righteous man?"' *(Lk.23:47)*.

Over the last two thousand years the rituals of faith, the words of tradition, the noblest of people who allowed grace to influence their humanity have built up a great reservoir of hope and a resource of incalculable value as we foster a faith appropriate to our age.

> *Being Christian is not an ethical choice or a lofty idea, but the encounter with an event, a person, which gives life a new horizon and a decisive direction.*
>
> *Deus Caritas Est Para.1.* Pope Benedict XVI